DATE

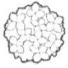

DATE

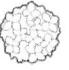

DATE

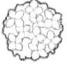

DATE

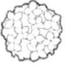

DATE

DATE . .

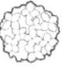

DATE

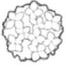

DATE

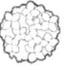

DATE . .

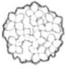

DATE

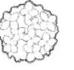

DATE

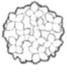

DATE

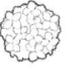

DATE . .

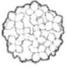

DATE

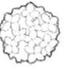

DATE . .

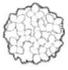

DATE

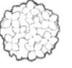

DATE

DATE

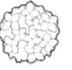

DATE

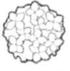

DATE

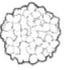

DATE

DATE

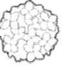

DATE

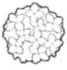

DATE

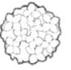

DATE

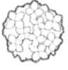

DATE . .

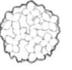

DATE . .

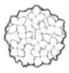

DATE . .

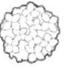

DATE . .

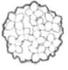

DATE

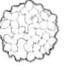

DATE

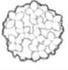

DATE

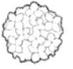

DATE

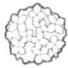

DATE . .

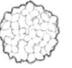

DATE · ·

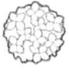

DATE . .

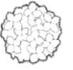

DATE

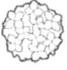

DATE . .

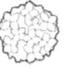

DATE

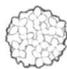

DATE

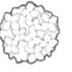

DATE . .

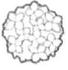

DATE

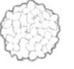

DATE

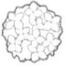

DATE . .

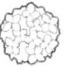

DATE

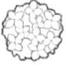

DATE . .

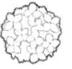

DATE

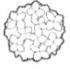

DATE . .

DATE

DATE

DATE

DATE . .

DATE

DATE . .

DATE

DATE . .

DATE

DATE

DATE

DATE · ·

DATE

DATE

DATE

DATE

DATE

DATE . .

DATE

DATE

DATE

DATE

DATE . .

DATE

DATE

DATE . .

DATE . .

DATE . .

DATE

DATE

DATE

DATE . .

DATE

DATE

DATE

DATE

DATE

DATE . .

DATE

DATE

DATE

DATE · ·

DATE

DATE

DATE

DATE

DATE

DATE

DATE